SWERVE

SWERVE

Sheri-D Wilson

Sheri-D Wilson
2003

ARSENAL PULP PRESS
VANCOUVER

SWERVE
Copyright © 1993 by Sheri-D Wilson

ARSENAL PULP PRESS
100-1062 Homer Street
Vancouver, B.C. Canada
V6B 2W9

The publisher gratefully acknowledges the assistance of the Canada Council and the Cultural Services Branch, Ministry of Tourism and Ministry Responsible for Culture.

THANK-Q TO: Dean Allen, Randy Bergh, David Cochrane, Babz Chula, Heather Elton, Eve, Lori Goldberg, Ladislav Guderna, Martin Guderna, Brian Lam, Micki Maunsell, Eric Metcalfe, Donna Miles, Gordon Murray, Julian Neil, Nien, Debra Penticoste, Barry Reynolds, Gabrielle Rose, Teri Snelgrove, Michael Turner, Sharon Thesen, and Bill Wilson.

Cover Design and Art Direction by Dean Allen
Cover Photo by Chick Rice

Edited by Sharon Thesen
Overseen by Gordon Murray

Printed and bound in Canada by Kromar Printing

CANADIAN CATALOGUING IN PUBLICATION DATA:
Wilson, Sheri-D
  Swerve

  Poems.
  ISBN 0-88978-274-1

  I. Title
PS8595 . I5865S9 1993   C811' .54 C93-091858-4
PR9199.3.W548S9 1993

CONTENTS

for me Ma

Remember when Bumblebees were the size of a loon
And our love was the distance between us and the moon, ma
Momento mori, mama, mama
Momento mori, ma
I'll call ya

These works are meant to be read aloud.

HUNG DRAWN
& QUARTERED

Hung Drawn & Quartered *was originally presented February 10, 1990 in the Performance Art Series at The Western Front, Vancouver.*

The Experiment: Present six players with a copy of the text, a budget, and a deadline. Each artist will work on their component of the piece separately and combine contributions the day before presentation. One rehearsal only.

The Players:	Michael Green	*Lord Trustworthy*
	Sheri-D Wilson	*Mea Culpa Carmen*
	Michael O'Neill	*Music*
	Martin Guderna	*Visual Art*
	David Cochrane	*Lights*
	Ivana Lasic	*3rd-Eye/Props*
	Gordon Murray	*Lookout*

Rewritten excepts were performed by Sheri-D Wilson and Michael O'Neill in Seattle at the 1990 Bumbershoot Festival, with direction assistance from Teri Snelgrove.

In December 1991 a new version of the piece emerged for One Yellow Rabbit's High Performance Rodeo in Calgary and a three-day XXX-Mas Solstice *event at Gallery 56 in Vancouver.*

The Players:	Michael Green	*Lord Trustworthy*
	Sheri-D Wilson	*Mea Culpa Carmen*
	Peter Moller	*Music/Sound*
	Martin Guderna	*Visuals*
	Blake Brooker	*Direction*
	Ivana Lasic	*Costumes/Props*
	Gordon Murray	*Lookout*
	Larry Jones	*Calgary Tech.*
	Mark Charnell	*Vancouver Tech.*

In July 1992 Hung Drawn & Quartered *was presented at The Works Festival in Edmonton, Alberta. The version that follows is closest to that presented in the last performance.*

Hung Drawn & Quartered is the erotic journey of two lovers. She, MEA CULPA, is myth–gatherer, who transforms from a dancer in search of her inner art to the figurehead of her body-ship. He, LORD TRUSTWORTHY, is captive-captain of his own emotional crucible. Together they circumnavigate shifting oceans of human bondage in their Relation–Ship. The time is simultaneous.

❧ THE FIRST SCENE OPENS...

The music begins and continues as a weaving soundscape throughout the piece. LORD TRUSTWORTHY enters slowly. He is naked, carrying an oversized story book on his back.

MEA CULPA CARMEN enters and moves toward the book. She slowly opens the first page and she blows away the ancient dust that has collected between the pages. We are aware that this book has not been opened for at least a millennium. The story begins as something outside of her, a bedtime story, or interplanetary gossip. But it swiftly zaps her into the first person...into the recognition of her own life.

MEA CULPA CARMEN

LORD TRUSTWORTHY

Musician

CIRCUS OF A THOUSAND RINGS I

Musician: *Circus of a thousand rings*
                The story begins…

MEA CULPA CARMEN:
Once upon a time…
I was alive
I was alive
I could change my clothes
Blow my nose
Embrace with my arms
My arms
And pinch with my toes
O Ya
I WAS WOMAN
The moon moved in time with my tide
I could sort through the long dark hairs
Of a fine tooth comb
I could dance : I could swirl: I could glide : Ya
I danced with my Salome Soul
In a circus of a thousand rings
With a drop of ylang–ylang between my lips
The kiss of the serpent stings
Spanish summer heat
Rippling adrenaline–lanoline
Up and down my sun hot spine
Treading on the deepest waters
Tarantella the finest line
O
The places, faces, the spaces I went to
But nothing was ever mine

I danced for the court
For kings and that sort
In a sanctum sky room with its pillars and dome
The walls gilt gold as the tongues of illiterate gods
Reflecting the movements of a heartless home
After my grande finale when breath returned to my pulse
I was the toast of the courtly scene
Reviews, royal invites, awards, shmooze–ing parties
What I possessed was the mystery of a dancer
I was the movement queen
I would spend my days preparing to dance
Among jewels, scarves and perfume
I would dream sweet dreams of the perfect death
The dance that would take me to my tomb
The roominate would tremble
My temple through and through
The thought that kept me alive
Was the Death Dance
I knew
I had
To do

LORD TRUSTWORTHY: *[he leaves book and moves*
Her perfume lets balloon go   *into his own pool of light]*
Balloon perfume
That thing I cannot name
I cannot understand, distant to my perceptions –
What was it?
She was so beautiful,
I could not touch

LIES

Pulling lies, all lies
From my legs, from my eyes, pulling lies
Bones rattle in my skin, can't find no soul within
JUST TIE YOUR SHOES LITTLE DANCER
AND BEGIN, AND BEGIN, AND BEGIN
Ha
Don't know where to begin
Can't find an opening in
Impossible to feel my skin
Can't move in
Or begin, bloody thin
Lies

Cyborg Woman
Can't move woman

Lies in behind
Lies in behind

My soul : Woman
Cyborg Woman : Machine : You see
It's not for me, it's for them,
Expectations them

They say dance : And I dance
They say smile : And I smile
They say move : And move
And I move, and move   *[He dresses throughout Lies segment]*

 My brother married a woman just like my mother
 What is it with intelligent men,
 who choose women they only want to look at
 My father, my brother –

I witnessed my mother compressed by my father,
My brother condescends to his wife
When I look into my own life, do I see…
Lipstick on ice
Lipstick on ice

Burned out of passion
Can't find no soul
I'm the ashes of desire
Each breath pays its toll
Can't feel my blood anymore
Lights too dim to see
When your guts are surrounded by lies
Then you've got nothing to be
In the mirror I see a body smear
Locked behind a skeleton key
Nothing to be : Nothing to be : Nothing to me

O Oedipus!

The roominate a–tremble
My temple through and through
The thought that keeps me alive
Is the death dance
I know
I have
To do
To do

Mother–lover–friend
I've never screwed a woman that I could talk to after–worlds
A woman I could tell the truth to, after, between sheets
I mean truth –
I don't know what I'd do, if I was real with a woman
I wouldn't know how to label it, how to log it

Probably be friends, and you can't fuck your friends
Or you run the risk of fucking up the relationship
I'm caught in the net of change,
Change I cannot make,
'Cause it breaks the image, of what I think I see
I am

Scares the shit outta me
Living with the preoccupation of death
Toxic thought
POISON
(Bing Bong)
Hello : O

Mummy, I adore thee
Your cyclic cloak of steam from sacred stones
Takes me back . . .
To sticks and stones and broken bones.
Moon Mum, I am your son
I haven't stepped on any cracks,
I haven't broken any backs.
I will obey you just as the angels do
Pull up anchor, float to your shores
Bottle fireworks, draw my sword.
I would turn backwards the sundial of time,
For you : Wow
There isn't anything I wouldn't do.
O Mother,
I want to build you,
Piece by piece, inch by inch
With my super Lego set
I want to Xerox your fingers and toes
I want to etch–a–sketch your mighty omni–presence
And color it with crimson crayolas, Prussian blue

I want you to take me to the zoo
I want you to play THIS LITTLE PIGGY
And I want you to tell me,
To tell me, Dear Mother
What O what should I do.
I have read every word of Moby Dick—
O, I want your breast
Great Mother
I want to lay my head
Upon your protective chest,
I want to crawl back inside your icono—womb
And rest,
Sweet Mum,
O, I want to rest

[He jumps into her arms and she
cradles him, she rocks him like a baby,
and she lets him drop to the floor]

POISON

Do—yes—do
The dance of death I have to do
Slow—moves—do
Moves that groove
Have—to—do
Move groove
Smooth
And as I am dying I will be dancing
And as I am dancing, dying
Perfect pas de deux, sans une, yes
And at that maker milli—mile
When life passes before my face
My art will greet my life as friend
Swan on the lake of grace, yes
The dance of death,
I have to do,
Yes.

A psycho jazz—core fusion performance art piece
With post—symbolic images called
THE ANCIENT TAMBOURINE SKULL DANCE
One chance,
My first last dance
No more lies, I'm taking control ...
Incense will burn
From a cross bone urn
Reams and reams of ribbons will turn
White noise will reign, death—masque will stain
The room—in—ate will trem—men—ate
Beating out the pain

Beat.
  Beat.
    Beat.
Tambourine will hyp–no–tize
Pomegranate seeds will tantalize
Sweat beads flick–flack–flick from a sword
That slashes judgement eyes
Damnation!
Dance trance dream lance
Footwork free to chance
Do–yes–do
Dance 'til death, a tai chi waltz
Pumice from dust until dawn
Yes Do.

      Waiting for change from my
      Inexorable preoccupation with destructive 'anti–matter' intimacies
      That delusively waver me from truthful associations
      Waiting for change to evolve me,
      To devolve me
      To stop those 'momentary madness' distractions and
      To lose enough self control, that I might love
      I want to grow up
      I must prepare my soul
      Prepare.

THE ANCIENT TAMBOURINE
SKULL DANCE

[She tells the story as she re−enacts the movements of The Dance of Death]

Preparation in place, as a shrine for a prayer
The day arrives smooth, without snag, nor snare
Ba−dum−bum, Drum
The hour to dance is drawing near
I feel the charge, the rush, the fear
The taste of poison is simple
Screams of terror, sans sound
The poison of lust, the lust of death
One last drink from my favorite goblet…
Well, lust doesn't actually kill you,
Poison does
One last sip from my favorite goblet…
My head begins swimming around
O, the undertow

I enter the stateroom with ease
Moves with a poisonous breeze
I know the arrows that sting me
Pomegranate and tambourine animate
Alive in each of my hands
Now, I feel like I'm holding the beach
Instead of holding the sand
My eyes meet the eyes of a king and they say
I AM HERE, ON MY OWN, COMMAND

I have heard of the other eyes watching
The ones sitting next to the throne
Lord Trustworthy the super star sea captain
The well−carved man, who is always alone

Magic bells jingle through my veins
Sparrows draw worms from my ground
A life time flashes by and by and by
Wade, wallow and drowned
O the undertow
Fire breathing lips the story of when and woe
Jazz beating hips, arrow from a p–p–poisonous bow
O Mercy
O The Undertow
Dancing, my last
      Dancing, my last
           Dancing my
Juices are turning and churning and burning
Lava spewing forth from an altered night–world
Nerves take to shaking
Trembling cold, bitter wind
Reeds reverb with the saints as they cry
Through the cracks of mind warp grins
Room distilled, turning tour de force
Like the inside corners of my
Brain
Eyes roll back
Berserk attack
Dragons before they are slain
The onlookers eclipse
Dissolve
Room revolves
Distorts
And is gone
Los Siento lace unravels
On darkness before it turns dawn
O THE UNDERTOW

Dancing, my last
      Dancing, my last
            Dancing, my last
Convulsing heels and castanets
Walls that crumble to their end
Illusions in the eyes of a black–quoted raven
Some holes are too large to mend

And at the moment of departure
The place between this world
And the next

Nothing

Nothing…

Absolutely nothing   *[She snaps her fingers]*

ANYWAY
I have reached the peak where I shiver with sweat
My insides are peeling from my outer skin
My bones are playing pins and needles
And death is dancing in
Slicing the pomegranate open
Like hell or a heart or a home
Between black and white pillars
Under a painted dome
Ha ha ha ha ha ha ha
CIRCUS OF A THOUSAND RINGS
And as my last breath retreats
As freedoms pass before my eyes
Lord Trustworthy has me sign a paper
And kisses my final ass Good–bye, Farewell
He says my body would be reconstructed
To place at the face of his ship

Because Trustworthy wants forever
To have me at his fingertips
The first time he touches me
He gets a sliver
Blood from the slave to the giver

The next thing you know I'm mounted
All carved and ready to sail
Looking frantically for the soul
That got caught, between the head and the tail
Caught between the wind and the gale
The movements that once filled my soul
Are stilted creaking and cold
GODS
I can't even see myself for looking
I want something to hold
I need to turn backwards the welling wheel of time
I want to uncommit the purpose of the perfect crime
So
Here I am a wreck on the front of a vessel called me
I want to see my breath circle the globe and return
I need my body to sink before I can feel it burn
I long to learn to dance
For myself
To feel the grass under toe
To release all my fears
To touch my own tears
To seed
To water
To grow
I don't know
This futile fertility
Usurped

Men enter and then they're gone
This thing that I call woman
This light that is here and beyond
COUP DE GRACE

> She challenged me, with her movements
> She mused me, with her eyes
> She saw me for a moment
> Without my well–rehearsed disguise.

> > *[Mea Culpa Carmen has transformed into the figurehead of a ship]*

NOW

Musician: *Now*
              We meet the night
              Fall
              Together

Now.
I'm Mea Culpa Carmen
I live in a world of sin
Orders were given to paint my decks red
To disguise the blood when the battle begins

If it does

There are some that call me Persephone,
Queen of the underworld
At sea
But I think Mea Culpa Carmen suits me better
It's a label of duality
Ha

I'm bound on a voyage of discovery
The flagship of Lord Trustworthy and his 500 men
Dealing with cards that were already dealt
On the ruddy decks, of way back when

Seabirds call above the cry of the wake
That I'm the most notorious of all known ships
With mean and best proportion, circumnavigating torso torsions
And thirty−two guns between secret seaworthy lips

I'm Mea Culpa Carmen
It took 3,000 oaks to fashion my skin
Before you, a floating forest
With sealed book pages and brandy within

The old–fashioned open air gallery
Is where the captain comes in the night
To attend my council waft and wheeze
To touch the aerodynamics of my freehold flight

Warm mist blowing up my billowy gown
Exposing my breasts' dripping sea
My body sipping the waters of Trustworthy's name
Blood is Mercury in sharp–shooting degrees

Wine–dark deep as the spell of Neptune's knot
Our bed moves in time with the tide
We speak through silent reflection to a mirror–altered perception
When you're a citizen of the world, there's nothing to hide, in Jekyll

So quarter the deck, draw my gestures in chain
Hang me on your mast, oh sea–stained mate
Arise from your sleep to dispel and to keep
The truth that does falsify our fate t . t . t .

TRUSTWORTHY HOLDS
ONTO THE NIGHT

[Lord Trustworthy is masturbating with an eleven–inch
flesh–coloured vibrator, singing the blues while he mock jerks–off]

Rockabye

Rockabye

Rockabye Blues

Sleepin's got me hood–winked

Twisting me supernatural screws

My hormones are on electroids

Fires got a hold of my hair

Jerking my head in and out of itself

A storm with no lightning, just doesn't seem fair

Engines of God

Rip through

One Two

Rip through

Lasso

My soul

Wrap it in a tissue

And stuff it in a little hole

Eyes light, lips cringe

Holding secrets, release of the pistol soul

Beat   Beat Heart Beat t . t . t .

Fingertips a–tingle

Face–up, sundown glow

Pissing moon stains into the night

Afterthoughts, go with the snow

I have heard the angels do Kama Sutra

With my luck I'll live forever

I don't know

Rockabye

Rockabye

Rockabye Blues

When there's no magic number

There's something to lose

One Two

One Two

Conjuring mind held in shackles

Growing pains about to explode

What I need is a sea horse to carry this

More than cumbersome load

The golden orbs are expanding

To an all–time spiritual high

Most amazing

An evil eye

Ha

I could see more than her reflection, if only

I could touch her lips, if only … if only …

O

I must be wind jammed

To be in love with a transported ship

If only I could run my foot up the inside

Of her well–turned wooden thigh

Why'd she have to do it

Why'd she have to die

Let go

Release, I tell myself

One Two

Let go, I tell myself

Let go

One Two

RAPTURE

GOD

[LORD TRUSTWORTHY *immediately falls into a deep and snoreful sleep*]

MEA CULPA CARMEN RESPONDS

DAMN
RAPTURE
Capture
Snap
My alarms resound like bad luck charms
When a seaman stirs within me, my ship, me
Restless liaison, no light house
Caught in the net between two separate worlds
The world Before Coming
B.C.
And the world After Coming   *[She looks down at him snoring]*
Wouldn't you agree
Ha
Melting sun rays in a moon−god V
Before me
Before me
Wrinkles on the water−skin
Throb−riff on an ancient sea
Begin.

Lord Trustworthy!−

DIALOGUE I

I'll be with you in a heart beat
Pa pum   *[he jumps on deck]*
You called

I heard you muttering
Were you talking to yourself
Down below?

To myself. Yes.
Do you still love me?

Yes madly.
And you me?

No.

I know.

What do you?

That you ...

That I ...

O nothing.

There she is, just coming up

My evening star

We're standing on the peak of a moonlit mountain
Inside the dregs of darkness

Veeee—ness

Search light luna
Night undresses and lunas
Legs fan
Stretch open
Venia
Night stretches, and salty skies
Open
To escape darkness.
Moon madness.

M'lord, what troubles you?
What brings you thus?

SLEEP WALKER

Unrest, m'love, unrest
My sea—deep troubled mind
Brain—Sick—Bow—Man
A coat that is aero—lined
Head lock gossip crawling
Up the leg to the loin, where it grinds
Master—ship over one's desires
'Tis the thing that makes you blind
For God's Sake
I killed a whale to see how it would feel
On the bloody shores of a mind—mad beach
Noble prey expire, a death whisper crier
In a frequency that shrills, in a single silent—

Beseech.

Toss and turn
Sweat and burn
Womb—Whined—and Whirl
Night blues, sweet love
Night blues
In a maze my mind doth swirl
Mea Culpa, Mea Culpa
I want you so madly
So goodly, so badly.
My salt for you is the wake where the Gods—Do—Soar
Love feast and ceiling wax
My mind is stapled to the floor
Somnambulist of reason
My constellations crack like a lash
Through the skin of Atlantis' creaking door

O

Unwilling to accept the barnacle dreams
Of my sudorific sleep
Amid clumsy emotions
And defenceless dagger notions
I arose to your voice
The salt sting song of a siren
With night shadows lapping toward me
As swordfish
I arose from sopping twisted sheets
And cast myself from the pool of succubus
Wounded by the wand of wanton
Wanton of what, I cannot know ... know not what
Ocean circulations
Expectations
Hallucinations
Incan ...
Palpa ...
To warm my cool night hands
On your crackling heart
Splinter kindling, love–signs apart
I rose to touch the muse of unrest
Unrest, m'love, unrest
I arose to tell you a tale
To take you in
To hold you in between, this place and sin
So throw me a life line
Mea Culpa
Carmen friend.

I want you now at 45 degrees
I'm standing dead center on a hairpin bend

DIALOGUE II

It's the games we play alone, you know

> I know

I know

> What do you?

That you ...

> That I?

O, Nothing

> No, what?

Well, it's just that, well, I think you should know that
According to the Yogis
Masturbating is really bad for you
They say that your nerve endings stay erect and don't calm down
For four hours which affects your creative center, your flow.
The old adage of blindness and hairy palms isn't far off, you know

> That's fine if you're living on a mountain top but I'm not about to
> Start doing Kundalini on deck.
> There'd be a mutiny.

Think of the creative energy that you're wasting.

> Think about Genet or Picasso,
> They couldn't keep their hands off themselves
> And I'll tell you something else, if I didn't have some release
> I wouldn't be able to concentrate on guilding this vessel.

Excuse me?

> Ga–zun–tide.

Who is guilding whom?

Indeed, yes, quite.

M'Lord, what are your dreams?
What direction does the face of your compass point?
What do you dream that keeps you awake, thus?

DREAM 1 OR TRUSTWORTHY DREAMS 1

Dreams
O yes
I remember now
It all starts with the Crowned King, called ...
Him,
And
One day as Him strolled amid the gardens of the Kingdom of Him,
He stopped to talk to his favorite Rhododendron plant,
You see, in this dream Him obviously mistook plants for people
Which is not to say that Him in turn mistook people for plants
Anyway, he, Him, spoke to his people through this plant,
And he, Him, proclaimed:
"That you and each of you
Be taken from whence you came
And from thence be drawn on a hurdle
To your place of execution ..."

Exaltation.

Exaltation?

Exaltation!

That's right.

Yea.

Exaltation, that's what he, Him, said in the dream.

Of course.

And there you shall be bound in a pillory
Naked   *[Said together]*
Warm winds,
Winds blowing in ringing spins, in spinning rings

And you shall be tormented by touch
On the nape of your neck
With sea urchin spines
And other things cool and wet
You shall not stir
Menacing any motion
In a stead—fast web behind spider—webbed bars
Caught on the fine line between two stars
Yet alive and basking in phoenix euphoria
You will watch through thirst as your lover disrobes
Potions on peach skin, tongue touch your ear lobe
Fingers dipped in clove oil
Will start at your toes
Slowly rise up your inner thigh
To the place of prose where passion goes

The moon moans

What truer alchemy than that which takes place on the anatomy?

Hum—m—m

And your skin will burn, as the spice of the sun
Your head will turn, has it finished or begun
You, unallowed to move, through a pleasure such as this
And you ask yourself,
Is this torture or is this bliss?
And your body will shake the four corners of the earth
And your insides quake, as an unsnipped babe at birth

Is this torture or is this bliss—

And Him proclaimed to the masses of Rhododendron:
"And Gods, have mercy, on our souls." Amen.

Woe—man.

Is there any compensation for criminal wrongdoing,
When it happens thus,
In one's mind?

Strange dreams,
What is the sentence for Mind High Treason?

Death.

Or boredom
If you're holding aces and eights,
You're starin' down on a dead man's hand
Bang.
Speak you, with premonition on your tongue, of Treason?

Of trees, of trees, criss−crossed for death
I speak to you of trees
I speak of dreams, that death might seize
I speak of Godly butchery
Fruitless hope
I can't find the sky, hiding
Behind a ring of rope
You're a floating forest nailed to my fly
I unbutton my want and I ask myself : Why?
When I alight to hear your body creak
My carnal need is driven to peak
For that which I cannot have
Jesus wept!
I keep running when I hear the word "Halt"
And it's my own damn fault
For creating you ...

What?   *[Wham! Musician hits drum, she rocks the boat]*

For creating ...

What?   *[Wham!]*

    You ...

WHAT?   *[Wham!]*

    For ...

                                               [Wham!]

    Creating ...

                                               [Wham!]

    Y O U ...
    Your signet branded on the palms of both of my hands

                                               [Wham!]

DAMN YOU, DICKHEAD!
How dare you speak of creation,
Souls are created in history.
There is a tribe of invisible women
Who move as shadows
Have you felt them in our presence?

    No

Walk softly, then.

    I have looked into the eyes of Troy.

Donahue?
O, really, did he look well?

    I have sipped opium tea with Sappho.

Opium tea?

    With Sappho.

I HAVE

I have dined with dinosaurs

Sleazed with snakes

Flown cross–continental, with an apex of eagles

And I have

Dived a thousand leagues, with the great whale people

I have heard in High Fidelity

I have eaten rhino raw

I have greeted anti–pescens on the beach playing Frisbee

And I have silenced what I saw

I have known silence

Memory and mystery

Wax works of horror and Niagara Falls

Man's life is worth a shilling

When the voice of mercy killing calls

I have known great sinners

The treasures of my life

Those who look for the future in oracles

Those who have loved me with a knife,

So

Beware the Tides of March.

The question is :

DID I CREATE YOU OR DID YOU CREATE ME?

Touché.

Point taken, m'ladyship.

DIALOGUE III: WELL

Well,
Night watch horizon
The clouds at dusk

> **Twilight**

Yes
Dusk

Before darkness falls

> **Stumbles**

Yes
Falls

The clouds are camels
Crossing the sky
Ocean
As a desert, I
A creaking cradle in the sand
The water colour is as haunting
As the thought of my womb on land
Can you count your enemies,
On the fingers of one of your hands?
The sun gods brand their anger
On my paint peeling face
Clouds try to comfort
With an arms length embrace
But tell me
When the mirage begins to erase
Will you break my fall from grace?

[They look at each other in an imaginary reflection below]

> Breathless trip from a dune
> Dwell I but in the suburbs
> Of your good pleasure? *[long silence]*
> Where will you die?

In my lover's arms
You see, there are limitations to every preordained
Legacy.

> At least we have the pleasure of speaking to one another
> In our reflection my face is pressed
> Against your mid–drift–ing

I hold you,
In the perfect silence of the sea

> The outer edges of the world
> Concentric nipples

Delphinium eyes

> Optical illusion
> The mirror is the mean difference

If we break this mirror
It will be more than seven years
For you to die with your mouth open
In a bed of blood blue tears
Blub Blub Blub

> Indeed

So indeed *[They laugh]*

DREAM II OR TRUSTWORTHY DREAMS II

A messenger arrives on his mountain goat
Through streets as narrow as minds
To the feast of Corpus Christi
Or, that's what it said on the sign
So, he's there
The messenger
And before him is a crypt of monks
All cloaked and bowing their heads
Ah
Ah
Ah
In the rising mist of incense
A phosphorescent dancer
Knows the words not necessary to be said
That's you
Spinning top
Dervish death dance
Spanish crystals flicker
From your sword, parlay coup de grace
Doing the ancient tambourine snake

Your beads sting the light
And your skin doth counter−current and claw
Black bustier and pomegranate
Seeds are what I saw
Eyes jet, with the poison of lust
From the flesh full fire of your source
Bending through your tendons
Trembling bells almost bending
Through the wilderness percussion
Of pre−remorse

One Two
One Two
Your first dance for me
Your last dance for me
One Two
The phantoms are frail against your sin−u−ee snake skin
Falling to your knees in a beatitude back bend
One bite from the last apple instead of the first
Mood rings made of eye paint have never been easy to end
The cool blue sword comes to rest on your chest
As your head turns up to the dome
Veins unravel as hair from a twist
Knotted nexus, in search of a home

Don't get rattled I tell myself
Don't
Don't
Don't get rattled
I tell myself
Don't get rattled
I tell myself
Don't get rattled
Don't get rattled
Don't
Get
Rattled rattled
Ra Ra Ratt
Don't get rattled
Don't get rattled
I tell myself
Don't get, get rattled
I tell myself
Don't

CIRCUS OF A THOUSAND RINGS II

The Circus of a Thousand Rings
I poisoned myself on the lips of a king
O my black soul
I was running before I learned how to crawl
I learned how to write before I learned how to scrawl
Gods, I wanted to love so I learned how to lust
My heart went to hell, my soul turned to dust
I burned my candles 'til there was nothing left of my wick
I used my tongue 'til I was all out of lick
Sad dance that turns our passion to stone
That makes us drift forever, on a sea of ever alone
Unlearn the game that has held me to the snake
Unlearn the truth along with the mistakes
My shell is weather beaten with change
And it always seems so strange
'Cause my insides turn like wind in a storm
And I know well it's not blankets that find us warm

Lord Trustworthy
Or whoever you think you might be
Throw away your log and hear a figurehead's decree
You delude yourself in thinking the last dance was mine or yours
The things that are most precious we hide away in drawers
The dance that enters the third parallel and beyond
Bird escapes the cage and swims into the dawn
Beast that moves with eternity on its heels
Has one extra second in the face of the turning wheel

I am a dance of me
I am the trunk of a tree
Count the rings
Coin collecting or density
Time scholar
Count the stillness
For that, is where, the treasures, be

DIALOGUE VI

> No dead heads in our path
> I think I'll go down below

Sweet dreams
Return thee in a solar day

> And in a stolen night
> I'm going knowing I can come back

DREAMGATHERING

Dreamgathering

    Worship

Dreamgathering

    Warship

Dreamgathering

    Dreamgathering

Ah

    Ah

Dreamgathering
Stones and shells

    Friendship

Dreamgathering
Bones and bells

    Courtship

Dreamgathering stem

    Seductionship

Broken dreams
Dream boat spell

    Relationship

Pool pell mell
Dreamgathering
Truth to tell
Pillow swell

Receivership

Slumbersinking

Hardship

Sound the bell

About ship

Dreamgathering
Slipped and fell

Abandonship

Drop like hell

Sunkin' ship

Down the well

Ship ship
Longest love beads I've ever seen

OVOVIVIPAROUS

I am the egg factory
On ember—red harvest moon, full of Pisces
A citrus flare, disk of Drudaria
Temple of blazing lionesses
At high noon
In the desert sun
Cunt out, fertility tears

I am the egg factory
Rhapsodized inner—most eyes
Deepening tones yielding, to lunas love—trance sighs,
It's a herd of stampeding buffalo, writhing and railing
Incensed with cosmic—craze, inside me
It's a herd of brazen bison
Performing their thunder—hooved primeval rites, inside me
Monad, super nova ova—flagellation, in my gonads meating site

O, I am the egg factory
Trouble tattooed on the inside of my thighs
Scent rising up sensitized and raw and roar
Pulsing paraselene, peacock screeeech
My heart jemba beats, tantric messages
Hor—moan—ing
My sun cracks the sky at dawn
Fore—boding
And I can't even leave my house, held hostage by an Ostrich
Egg
Ready to give birth, inside me

I am the egg factory,
Free ranging furnace factory
A HUMAN popcorn popper, ovoid popcorn popping and
Shaking, and vibrating explosions, wailing to the moon—air popcorn, pulse

I am the fallopian fly strip danger zone
Frenzied by the flies I attract, by the spell of
My lunar lamppost cries—Swat, Swat
Get away you flies, get away you flies
Or you die, flies.
OR YOU DIE.

I am the egg factory
And in case you're wondering
It is not a biological clock tic—talking : O No.
It's the universe shaking me down
Jonesing and jostling, lambasting me with my own confused visions of
Love
It's the universe converging its hard hat and rubber gloves special effects
Mentality on me—In me …
Shaking, is a cunt
Aching, is a cunt
Throbbing for pheromones, while standing on my head is a cunt that's
Weeping for intimate mantra
Waiting, waiting for the Union leader to telegraph my eggy factory with
Her meditation, of peace.

> Peace.
> Forty taels of silk,
> Bolts of satin and damask silk yarn
> Sable and ermine skins
> Brocade, woven garments, a half fathom of satin ribbon,
> Eaglewood, for Christ's sake,
> Gold dust and pearls, quicksilver
> Vermillion, clove, ginger, indigo, honey, beeswax, sandlewood, musk
> And still, I can't have you
> You're not at all in the image of my mother, but
> I love you.

THE STORM

I call the wind
To begin
Pull my wings, Rap—ture
Shake my timber, Trap—lure
Cap, current and rocking chair
Tonight the dance of ember flare
With clenched eyes and open fist
I can feel before me the rising mist
I conjure the sea to gargle its throat
Command singing fish to reach a hypnotical note
Slowly sea
Unlace all myth
Toward me
Toward me
Ruu wings, sweet water, spirit delight
Celestial magic blast
Through such a night o nights
Illuminate the wonder
Stampede hooves of thunder
Beating boron under earth
Synergy flexing muscles
Pearls unleashed at birth
Yer
Yer
Riding crop and flambé wall
Let me enter your eye
For there my blood doth call
Clouds of lightning
Let me dance
Let the waters boil
A perfect romance

Slowly with spinning world outside my sphere
Rock the rolling motion none can steer
Ha
Sailing headlong into the eye of a storm
With open sail
I'm being pulled by screams, direction in braille
Take me
Chariot to the underworld
Where live no tricks
No sticks, no crucifix
Hello Atlantis
My preying mantis
Ropes unfurl
Knots uncurl
Hammocks are left in a spin
Hearts pumping tidal waves
I am coming in–
Your scent still holds me
From when I loved you a century ago
I bask
I bath
To the fertility sea
Wild and slow
O
I make three wishes.

     O
     Earth is moving
     One
     Two
     Three

Eyes
Pushing

Enveloping
Soul shadows and shock waves
I can hear the earth quaking
Storm is breaking
Freedom to all living slaves

     Hell's bells are raging
     My charts blew out to sea
     ALL MEN TO THEIR STATIONS
     I THINK SHE'S SACRIFICING ...

Sha bang
Sha bang
I can hear the crowsnest calling

     MONSTERS AHEAD, UPRISE
     SHAFTS OF STONE GULPING   *[She laughs]*

All hands to save Mea Culpa from dancing us to our grave
I can feel
The feet of men a'scurry
Termites tickle within, the fury
O the fury

     WE'RE TAKING ON WATER!
     CUT AWAY THE MASTS
     JETTISON EVERYTHING ON DECK!

Grown men atop my tomb
Dancing within my spinning womb
Record breaking, pails of power
Into the face of the flower
STORM!

STORM!
Heavy breathing ocean gales have gotten their
Grappling hooks into our skin!

Drums pound
Psychedelic sea—
Resound

Raze the deckhouses and upper works
From stern to stern

Face beating and saturate
Skin tears lacerate
The mirror combusted
Breaking her mask
Shards of sea
Eyes break free
Sha bang
Sha bang

Don't get rattled, I tell myself
Don't get rattled
Wait! Mea Culpa!

SHARDS DO LACERATE!

Flyer
Splice the cables and clinch them into anchors
Rocks up ahead, rocks, rocks up ahead
TURN ABOUT!

Hold me ocean in between
The broken rings and ties
Help me escape the grey mystic knotted net
And fly,
On the backs of quasars

Fly
As a new found god
From the shores of cinder sand
Purple
Purple
Purple
Take me

    Wars of emotion

My breasts swell with salty milk
My soul parts as the finest silk
Temple shrine, burning chime
The Delphi delivers one last—
Yes.

       Mea Culpa
       Lover—friend
       Storm with an eye
       We shall live
       Where we shall die
       For
       Mea
       Ever

Ever.
I can hear a familiar voice
Gathering us in her vision.

TABOO X TWO

Taboo X Two *was first performed at the 1989 Edmonton Fringe Festival and at Open Space in Victoria, B.C.*

The Players: Harold Gent *Boeing Bird/Music*
Sheri–D Wilson *Salmon*
Evelyn Roth *Alter–Salmon/Designer*
Gordon Murray *Overview*

In February 1993 a new version of the piece emerged for a one night performance in a swimming pool for Alberta Theatre Project's Out of Bounds Series.

The Players: Sheri–D Wilson *Boeing Bird/Salmon*
Peter Moller *Music/Sound*
Babz Chula *Direction*
Gordon Murray *Overview*

The version that follows is the original text.

TABOO X TWO speaks in the language of the birds. She, the SALMON, follows the most importand life urge, to spawn. DR.Q captures her and takes her back to the lab where he is running tests on her. He, BOEING BIRD, born from a slot machine in Las Vegas, is desperate to contact the voice of the salmon who he is channelling. The time is simultaneous.

❀ THE FIRST SCENE OPENS...

With Boeing Bird flying across the stage with his concord imitation. He lands on one of the tree tops to speak/entertain the audience he has spotted. There is a sound score that runs throughout the piece.

The Salmon enters swimming through the air as if she were underwater. She is doing a parody of a fish swimming underwater.

The key word here is CAMP, and I do mean IT UP.

BOEING BIRD

SALMON

VOICE OF AUTHORITY

BOEING BIRD:

Veroom...

Eerrch...

Veroom...

Eerrch...

Veroom...

Eerrch...

5 – 6 – 7 – 8

THE JUJUJIVE JABBER JAM

And blast off
Through the clouds
Busting loose to the stars
Shooting stars, to the moon
Curving around comets, astral bodies, and beyond

Yo – mmm – good – O – YA!
Flying with ease and a cool self assurance
Surfing through wind waves
Riding the air currents

Yo – mmm – good – O – YA!
A new relationship
Is like freshly washed hair
Oooo it feels so good
But you know when you comb, you'll find a snare
Time to condition: time to tame

Yo – mmm – good – O – YA!
I'm running out of breath from all this flying
Better stop and energize my jets
I'm beginning to feel like the practise ball
For the New York Mets

Duende Duende Duende Duende
Coming in for a landing
Air traffic controls under wing
Sensations feel so good
So good, they almost sting.
Sting
Sting

I spy the treetops now
Landing gear down and ready to clear
Check Check Check
objects in the mirror are closer than they appear
Zoom—lens view
The avenue is lined
With the heads of bald eagles
Sun lighting crowns
Majestic rhapsody of regal
I call them the hairless angels
Receding relics with wings

Yo—mmm—good—O—YA!
Runway strip
My landing point
The summit tip
Of a sharp—edged cliff
Overlooking the open sea
The humans call it Lily Point
But it will always be Club Fabulous to me
Yo—ya!
Club Fabulous is more than Lily Point
Or the branch arm of a mountain Oak Tree
It's a Holy Land
A tantra God
It's a sanctum seduction institution sublime

It's the key—
It's Cools—ville incorporated
It's Saturn's sensational fantasy city
But most of all . . .
It's basically anything you desire it to be
Club Fabulous is an esoteric galaxy!

So, what I'm saying is . . .
It's the perfect place to stop and digest
The most extraordinary thing that happened to me
Today
So extra—ordinary was this thing
That I believe it may well have changed my life
I know it's a little early to tell yet
But there's one thing for sure I can say
I
Feel
Different
Weird things are happening
I know I look like the same old Boeing Bird
Born from a slot machine in Las Vegas
But things are definitely twisted here
I feel like the bloody Goddess Mut
Pouring water of life from the sycamore tree
Call it a make over
Call it a psyche cleaning
Call it a re—built engine
Call it a Chakra scrub
Call it Boeing Bird
Iguana guy
Soul Searchivist
Light activist
Call it a wonder drug

Perhaps it was the Chips Ahoy chocolate chips that dunnit
I dunno
Crumbs to hallucinate
Chips to contemplate

SALMON TALE

Sonic Sacramanna
Sonic Sacramanna
Sonic Sacramanna
In the city of the sea
Sapphire aqua−marine
Blood from the milestone tree.
Birth was a marvelous invention
I'm glad it happened to me at sea
I'm told by my elders my first words spoken
Were "Buy me an RRSP"
I remember the first time I opened my eyes
Under water mandala floodlights
As far as the eyes could see
Silver−Blue−Sock−Eye Salmon
Born with the sky violet at twilight
I know it sounds a little far−fetched
But the water took possession of my skin, through that night
When I was young I liked to play in danger−zones
Alone at 2,000 fathoms diving deep and crazy and free
Sporting 3 D underwater glasses
I had everything that your typical clean scale guppie family
Of guilt−ridden affection could give me
Could supply
One happy well−adjusted salmon
Looking for answers in the sky
Sonic Sacramanna
In the urban center of the sea
It was like I was living a fairy tale dream
I even sang with the undersea rock band called The Marine Supremes

STOP FISHING IN THE NAME OF LOVE
BEFORE YOU CATCH MY HEART
THINK IT O–O–VER
Really deep,
Water songs
And other things

Once
I waited still in the water
Still cold
Still listening
To the beat riff of the waves lapping
I thought I'd try it 'cause I met Krishna Merdie
And he told me to find peace within myself
Without the gift wrapping

Anyway,
I was still
In the water
Listening away the day to the sound of the waves
And the story they had to say
When I heard the softest whisper
"Sshhh, Sshhh, Hey, Hey"
I turned to the sky behind me
And refracted in the white wash water up above
I saw the northern lights rushing across the sky
I heard the sound of lights lashing the tail feathers of the innocent dove
Dish water liquid, love
Dish water liquid, love
And, at that nano–second, I could hear
My own fish blood moving
Inside my veins
Rushing, pushing, calling, swerving
And cutting, quick changing lanes

Jing, Jing, Jing
Spraying forth a blood–stained rain

Again
I looked back to the sky action stars
And it seemed like the first time I had ever seen such a cluster
Of ancient soothsaying Czars
Where had they been?
I caught my Zen laughing to the sound of star sitars
But that night everything was so clear
And I thought...
The stars are the same distance from me as I am from them
Something bizarre has happened to me here
Well, peace is tricky business
What with all that suppressing all that anxiety
Like the cannery, or the politically correct,
Anglers, fishing nets or phone bills
And various other forms of frustrating
Free–ways
Suppressing anxiety peace
Sonic Sacramanna
In the city of the sea
Trying to swim to the center of the earth
If only...
If only...

THE COHO CAPTURE BY
DR. Q. RAPTURE

Rico – Chet   Rico – Chet
Rici – Co - Ho – Chet

Rico – Chet   Rico – Chet
Rici – Co - Ho – Chet

Rico – Chet   Rico – Chet
Rici – Co - Ho – Chet

Information, death by sea
Interrogation, cross examination, death by sea
Concentration, one naked bulb
Stapling me to a statistic, in a bubble gum machine

Rico – Chet   Rico – Chet
Rici – Co - Ho – Chet

Vesica–Piscis–Karma
I never saw Hells Gate or Goldstream
Vesica–Piscis–Karma
I am but a pawn in someone else's startling dream
Yeah, I live in a glass house tank, and sister this ain't no short–lived prank
In reality, I never saw Goldstream
Nor the movements of my shooting tail
Currents shallow and heat, swallow and Blue Heron.
I live like petrified driftwood
In a state of perpetual sleep
O, did I say state?

I meant province
In a province of perpetual sleep
Sleep
Kundalini

I was first upstream while I lasted, swimming with fervor and power
Fighting the winding course of Mount Purgatory's life−giving tower
Fish ahead of its time burning through the dawn
To meet my cosmic maker
To reach my peak and then spawn
To spawn,
O to spawn

To reach my peak and then spawn.
But between the moment of departure and that left behind
Something scooped me from my mission, closed my eyes, closed my mind
I was captured by a scientist
Let's call him Dr. Q
Dean of discipline and disaster
Repairing damaged souls with Elmer's all−purpose glue
This Q is a concoction creature
He has lived his life through a test tube and a beaker
He's a freaky little rimbo
Posing as a serum seeker
And I, a simple salmon, swimming in an oil slick
In search of a water based solution
Solution−Soluble−Slick−Solution
I never met the mouth of Goldstream's absolution
Dash−Pollution−Period
HOW THE HELL CAN I FIND A ROUTE OUTTA THIS MESS
POISONOUS : LAUGHING AT ANYONE'S EXPENSE
I feel like the spirit of Carmanah's largest tree
Trying to dodge McBlow's bloody ax−orcise
What?

In a restless pool of probing
In a glass house that's half my size
It's pinching me,
They're lynching me
With Silvo words and speechless sight
It curls my scales, makes me feel like, my skin
Is two sizes
Tighter than tight
Night in the kingdom of shadows
Kite that was never flown
I HOPE THERE'S NO HARD FEELINGS says Q
Through the walls with a lethal leer
THERE'S JUST A FEW MORE TESTS WE HAVE TO RUN ON YOU
HERE
No Q
No feelings at all, through blue
The spheres cracking in half
     No water
I'm pinching myself in church so I don't dare laugh
     No water
The stress of the hyaena panic button
Fire water brook time blues
Onion perfume
Honey smelling doom
Fertility spray up my nose like flower catz
Sweet mercy,
AND I DON'T FEEL A THING.
And the walls of this here glass house
Are closing in real fast
If you put a fish in a holding tank
I wonder how long it will last?
Sometimes, I
Almost feel hu–man

Sometimes I almost feel
Human
Sometimes,
I almost
Feel
Oui
But I don't like hawks.

BOEING BIRD TRIES TO
REACH THE SALMON

Duende Duende

Duende Duende

My suffering soul is escaping out of the top of my Boeing Bird Brain!

For it seems there lives a Salmon who is slowly going insane

I feel the glass walls, closing in on her real fast

I suppose it would be considered channeling

Tuning in, like a celestial reporter

Black Jack

Spin of fortune

Flash your esoteric luck

Jack–pot, crack–pot

Time to tune in again

Change the channel

I feel like a television set–sub set

Channeling

Channeling

Channeling radio–waves

Radio–active

I remember this time someone with crystal earrings

Came up to me on the strip

And asked me if they could read my palm

I mean, how absurd, I'm a bird!

Ooooo, I'm so easily distracted

Channeling

Channeling

I do hear voices, you know

And they kind of influence how I think

Give me ideas, or take ideas away, mostly

Remember earlier

When I told you that weird things have been happening?
Or did I say that to someone else?
Someplace else?
Some other time?

Anyway, it's weird...
I have been hearing the voice of a salmon
Who I have affectionately named Eye
It's no lie, I believe I can actually hear this Salmon Eye
The only problem seems to be
The question of whether she's tuned in on me
I would like to think that it's clear sailing channels between us
But she doesn't seem to hear me
Her voice has become more and more faint and distant
And I do believe she could well be in critical danger

If only...
There were some way to connect with her
Then I could teach her how to fly
She could escape,
Lay her eggs,
My dear invisible friend the Eye
And then die.

Yo Eye, do you read me?

BOEING BIRD AND THE
SALMON AT ODDS

Poetry Pollution

> You're coming in loud and clear
> Do you read me?

> I guess that means no.

Poetry Pollution
That's what I have on the inside of my brain
Poetry Pollution
Contaminated processed thoughts, city dweller stench is enough
To drive me insane
Poetry Pollution

> Can you hear me?

Rise out of the waves poison mist
Like S.O.S. sky fusion smoke signals
Air O's Air O's
Float above the greatly feared
Poof, it disappeared
Wild–der –nesssssssssss

Poetry Pollution
Sugar substitution
Bill of Rights
Or the constitution

Poetry Pollution
Decomposition : Decay

Poetry Pollution
I can't go on like this
Revolution

My brain is expanding and contracting
Solution expression
Exposition
Shun

Looking face to face at the barrel of a gun
Underwater poetry pollution
In the ocean
Shun
Bubble Bubble

Put the wilderness behind bars
Put sacred intelligence in jars
Pickle it and call someone's bluff
Clear cut, slash burning and other fancy stuff
Slogans in the glass house
Focus my wits
To avoid the execution chamber of my sleep
I have to keep moving, must move,
Must keep moving
Perpetual motion

Wait, whose thoughts are these?
Where is this coming from?
What am I saying
Think tank
INSOMNIA

SIMULTANEOUS

Eeeeee Gods!
There must be something that I can do

Insomnia

Synchronize our sundials and time lapse through
There must be some way I can communicate

Insomnia

I mean, if she's still alive

Insomnia

If she ever was alive
I mean, how can you tell?
Shadow making brain waves

Insomnia

Everything is simultaneous

Insomnia

Everything is simultaneous

Insomnia

Everything is simultaneous

Insomnia

Echos from the bottom of a wishing well
Well wishing, wishing well

Insomnia

No matter
Anti matter

Anything that moves is fair game
Hunt or be hunted
A fins−a−fin
Postcard

Postcard

Perhaps I'll write a postcard
Before I'm so zooney the roof of my womb escapes

An escape postcard to the other side

Yes, to soothe my muscle pumping brain

Yes
Yes
Yes

POSTCARD TO MY INVISIBLE FRIEND

POSTCARD TO MY INVISIBLE FRIEND I:
It's a stormy night tonight and cymbals sound like tubular
Bell thunder
Around the clock
Bright bangles and helium balloons
Both sides of the coin
Casino of life
Poetry pollution

POSTCARD TO MY INVISIBLE FRIEND II:
As psychically transmitted to my dear friend
The Eye
Who is standing by
Through tele—medium
BOEING BIRD
Born from a slot machine in Las Vegas
And who will attempt to telegraph my memory bank riff
And fast forward it to the eyes
Air tight
Mind lock
Jack pot brain
DING DING DING

The Delphi dimension connection
Interplanetary talking D—range
Long distance telepathic mind warp
DING DING DING

Three in a row
Hello? Hello? Hello?
Damn
Poetry Pollution

POSTCARD TO AN INVISIBLE FRIEND III:

Whom I cannot see
Ever.
Ever.
Ever.
Ever.

SALMON SUICIDE NOTE

Dear Death:
Lookin' for a little relief inside my outside inside brain
Feel like I just caught the last train to Emerald City
Coasting 'til the party is over and the animals are in their berths.
I didn't have anywhere to go
So I'm here at the bat–tank glass–house
Looking for the crumbs the rats left behind
Wondering where the hell I put my sane powder
To sprinkle away this mental D–rangement mind.
I feel like I just got licked by the cat that clawed me
And I'm tryin' to remember what I'm tryin' to forget
Tryin' to tell the difference between that and regret
And there must be more, my friend, there must be more.
DON'T SWIM OUT OF LINE, YOUNG LADY
Says Q, tryin' to tell me howta see my views
And my only response is blown and sounds like the tune–town drag
I'M NOT YOUNG, I'M NOT A LADY, AN' I DON'T SWIM IN LINE
SO SOMEONE'S WRONG ON ALL ACCOUNTS
Lady finger
Fish finger
Wait for the cold–blood to linger.
Friend, let us compare –
Paranoias:
I looked at myself in the glass house
And before me was a monster
I said "Hi monster face, how ya doin' this mornin'?"
And my face looked back at me and said
"Fine."
Tie a rope around my neck
To remind me to do the laundry
Lady finger

Fish finger
Wait for the cold–blood to linger.
I once met a fish who actually believes
That she can turn Salmon into a Human
And that the Salmon actually believes that they are Human.
O SAND
WHAT IS THIS POISONOUS DISPOSITION THAT WELLS INSIDE ME,
I FEEL SEPARATE FROM MYSELF LIKE I'M STANDING BACK–TO–BACK
WITH MYSELF.
I am a Blue Heron
Calling the Aztec wing–bat blues to you
Distant shore
To you, calling the Aztec wing–bat blues
I am a worm
Weaving you a power coat
Of the world's most treasured silk
I am a new mother
With ripe tit full
Unearthing for you, the taste of the sweetest milk
I put my ear close to the bottom of the tank
To see if I can hear you through the wilderness underworld
I put water and moonlight together
To bring you a string of galaxy pearls
I am a killer whale, swimming to freedom
I am a rooster, turned to steel
North South East West
I am the 7,000 deadly sins
And every sensation that they feel
I am everything un
And everything real
I am a raven, without a cause
I live by a guidebook of outlaw laws
Underwater spears pierce me

In the want of seeing you
To waltz
O to waltz, a slow—winged adage
What night is this that cannot see
The tender hooks that scar the spirit of trees?
What day being captured in a spiral of black light wave
Too late for penny—wells or wishbones or sacred hearts to save?
I want to stroke your Mars with the mask—task of my speculation
I want to touch your armour with a tingling sensation
I want you to shiver with the chill of the night's still air
I want, you to look, like you really mustn't care
O, say you recognize the feel of my skin
And my rhythm will break down in
The dense of the night.
But Hey, we got clean Chakras
So everything's alright.

Tonight
Observe history
Through a single star
Without speaking
Learn about the star
Evolve with the star
Until you heat the globe a thousand miles away
We are one
We are each other at once
Now I can see what you look like
If you were me seeing me see you
Your sounds
Your merry—go—rounds
Your perspective—collective
With mine.

Fly.
My fish friend, Eye
Fly!

What?
Who said that?
One voice speaks
I did
From outside inside you
Somewhere to the north
Of behind.
Yours Truly,
The Salmon

Friends, the Eye is standing by but does not read my thought

THE BOEING BIRD WRAITH WRAP

I wish it distinctly understood that I neither affirm nor deny the existence of psychic and spiritual phenomena, because it would certainly be taking on too much territory for me to refute statements made by Sir Oliver Lodge, Sir William Crookes, Russell Wallace, Professor Hyslop, Sir Arthur Conan Doyle and hundreds of other professors in various seats of learning, who all affirm that our dead do communicate with us through raps, automatic writing, mediumship, ghosts seen materialized in the flesh, speech through trumpets, the levitation of heavy bodies, and the removal of the sleeves off the shirts of mediums whose hands are held by skeptics.

        The time has come not to refute the scientists
        But to separate the wheat from the chaff
        The real from the unreal
        The skeptic from the septic
        So, we know what to believe
        Or not.
        Be careful what you think, or say
        The walls have ears
        And let me tell you, they're looking for something to hear.
        Now, to bigger business
        Now that we have resolved any skepticism about communication with
        the other side
        One rap means YES
        Two raps mean NO
        Three raps YOU'RE OUT!

        EYE, KINDLY ANSWER IF YOU HEAR ME

        Seance baby!

        EYE, KINDLY ANSWER IF YOU WILL COMMUNICATE WITH US

*[One rap is heard but really it is the sound
of the Salmon accidently running into something]*

Friends, Eye Is Here!
EYE, KINDLY ANSWER IF IT IS POSSIBLE FOR YOU TO GET
IN TOUCH,
DO YOU HEAR ME?!?

[One rap is heard, once again made accidentally by the Salmon]

Friends, that means YES!
It's magic
Abra–ca–da–bra
Candle–la–bra
Genuine psychic phenomenon!
EYE, MY DEAR FRIEND, WOULD YOU LIKE TO LEARN TO FLY?

Yes.

It's a wrap, friends, the real thing
Eye, we have a world between us, the world in a spin, within
Shared visions, wildlife and a truffle at the house of sin
Nature's orchestra is warming up and we will walk right in
The flying lesson
Cha–cha–cha

*[Boeing Bird teaches The Salmon to fly a la ballroom dancing style, but they remain
on different areas of the performance space. They jam]*

SALMON FLIES

Fish—two—ish—shun sizzle
Fish—two—ish—shun sizzle
INSIDE MY HEAD I'M FLYING
BUT MY BODY WILL NOT MOVE
INSIDE MY HEAD I'M FLYING
BUT MY BODY WILL NOT MOVE
My desirous scales are a talking feather
Speaking fish wing updraft and sky groove
Sky groove, higher, sky groove desire, higher
Sky groove
To spread my wings
And sky groove
Why fly, fair feather friend
Why fly

You are a hawk
Boeing Bird
Boeing Bird
I'll swim close to the surface
Eyes alert open to see
And you like a blanket of protective death
Would swoop down on me
Clutching your sharply filed talons
Into my bright silver skin
And as if to step off air
You lift off
Hitch hike
And Begin!

My spirit torch song moves
Upward so far I see earth
And back to my sacred spawning ground

Back to the conception of my Razzberry birth

Jazzberry Razzberry Jazzelberry Birth
Razzberry Jazzberry Razzelberry Birth

INSIDE MY HEAD I'M FLYING
BUT MY BODY WILL NOT MOVE
INSIDE MY HEAD I'M FLYING
BUT MY BODY WILL NOT MOVE
I cannot possibly fly
Embalmed
Toxic
Alloy
To die
Uninscribed and alone
Zone
Move!
Scare crow doing seminar
Spelling grave sight in the air
Fuck, the birds do it
Why can't I
Free–dom
Just doesn't seem fair
There must be 900 lives screaming inside me
I can feel each one like little time bombs ready to blow
I must get to the spawning ground
To release
To spill
To let go
Slooow fall
INSIDE MY HEAD I'M FLYING
BUT MY BODY WILL NOT MOVE
INSIDE MY HEAD I'M FLYING
BUT MY BODY WILL NOT MOVE

The Gods open Hellsgate and I swim right in
I dance right in
I move slow against the currents
Hanging tight to every wild cat white water rapid
Gushing
Swelling

And there is no knot in my veins
My strength opens wide open throttle
And I connect with the flow
And it spins me furiously in the air
Jumping, hurling
Spiraling
Tail sweeping me twisting and contorting
Gushing to the shape of a wild phantom
Fathom the flow
Fathom The Great Out Doors
Fathom G.O.D.
The Great Out Doors
Whistling past my sonars like bullets
Sonar free
Sonar free

Spilling myself up Goldstream
Steam out of the engine full speed ahead
No scars and full of life
Ready to spill into the trench
One last push into crystal madness
Thinking water secrets, blinking water eyes
French love
Red word passages peaking
Thy, will be done
In jazz snapping fingers
Pointing to the only witness

INSIDE MY HEAD I'M FLYING
BUT MY BODY WILL NOT MOVE
INSIDE MY HEAD I'M FLYING
BUT MY BODY WILL NOT MOVE
Hell!
Where are the burial rights?
Fossils fixed to a stony night
Vision quest indigo eyes
Pumping Driving Spilling Catching
Funnel vortex flies—
Mate struggle beside me
Through the tunnel home
Timing heart beats connected
To each other like ancient sitar strums
In a world of contradiction
In a world of Health Food and Tums
Together We Strive
Swimming tartar
Crepe de Chine
Flesh and soul

You and I together
Crazy fate keeping us whole
We're crazy, man
We're completely outta our trees
We're fighting for 900 lives in my gut
You and me
Totem and turn
Flurry and fern
Fin feather fly

Okay baby it's do or die
I fly
Soooooooow
Loooooooow

[She flies]

[And she lands and is faced with the Voice of Authority]

HALT WHO GOES THERE

It is I, the salmon

HALT WHO GOES THERE

It is I the salmon

TURN BACK

But I can't, I've come to spawn

TAKE ONE MORE STEP…

But I must spawn, there's…

AND I SHOOT!

*[She takes a step, she is shot, and as she dies,
she cries: "Sundial threatened by Time"]*

SUNDIAL THREATENED BY TIME

Tonight I burn my red candle for you in the wax
Last
Of your leaving.
Waiting for night to trip and fall into position
Into position
Into position
Into.

Your skin's got drops of perspiration
Glossing it over with little white lies
And I take a breath of you in
My fire
It's burning for you at this late hour mansion
Of my soul
Drenched in passion
Languid in lustre
Absorbed in the alabaster smooth
Of your skin.

Motion moving through my mind strings
Mind strings, through my mind strings
Through the segue inside my solar nexus
Golden section heart beat wakes up the dead
With great blows to the mortal soul
Ghosts cry cumulus sky
Ghosts sky cumulus cry
Drum, speaks in the cry, of the heart
Sounding off in the veins

Between the bones
Between the muscles
Between the nerves
Between.

Bones and muscles and nerves
Mind crawling and intertwining
Up the wall,
Cavalry call
Tower of inching illusion
My head lives inside the mouth of a cannon
My insides are trying to break out

And I take a breath of you in
And for the first time I smell the Zeysing of a lover
And I hold you inside me
And I gently breathe you out again
And we mix together as gods, ghosts, decagons
Ha.

I like the tiny lines at the corner of your eyes
And your eye ball blaze
I got you fixed tightly in my brain
And my temperature begins to rise
I feel the jazz, the jig–jag of electric currents
On the inside of my thighs
And oh the temperature
Oh the temperature
Oh the temperature, does she rise

Hey hey said the dragon as she opened her legs
I got the jungle
I got the oasis
I wanna mix with them, them,
I wanna mix with them ...

Tonight I burn
Burning a slow deliverance
How many centuries has it been

Tonight I burn my red candle for you in the wax

Last

Of your leaving.

Do you hear the heart beat of the wind in the street

       Question

What ever happened to Allan Fey

       Question

What are you thinking

       Question

Now

       Question

Where is the turpentine

       Question

Who gave the final order

       Question

Who gave the final

       Question

[She dies]

NOT A VICTORIAN WEEPER

[She rises]

Imagine yourself as a salmon
Imagine yourself as a bird trying to channel a salmon
Imagine yourself as the salmon getting captured by scientist Dr.Q
Imagine yourself as a bird trying to channel a salmon in a desperate
attempt to save the salmon's life
Imagine yourself as a salmon trapped by Dr.Q who channels a bird who
teaches you, the salmon, to fly
Imagine yourself as a bird attempting to telepathically teach the salmon
to fly out of the science−lab−holding−tank back to the sacred spawn-
ing ground where she was first captured by Dr.Q
Imagine yourself as a salmon, full of eggs by this time, learning aero-
dynamics telepathically from a bird, escaping the science lab via air
waves back to your spawning ground in a death−defying attempt to
save nine hundred screaming salmonides inside you
Imagine the spawning ground now owned by a multi−national corpora-
tion
Imagine yourself as the salmon looking down the barrel of a gun and
being told you can't enter your sacred spawning ground
Imagine yourself entering the spawning ground anyway and being shot
down
Imagine your death song
Imagine yourself singing that death lament
Imagine the sound of such a song, for nine hundred lives
Close your eyes, and
Imagine what might happen next

POEM-O-LOGUES

from *Sin City*

SIN CITY

Yesterday I went to my favorite sweet place called
NOT JUST DESSERT
Remember yesterday, scorching hot ...
I wore my little white linen frock.
And well,
I was sittin' at NOT JUST, having my usual –
Apple crumble pie à la mode
Covered in chocolate cheesecake
With a mocha coffee double decadence
Pineapple–strawberry fruit shake.

And well,
I was sittin' there in Breakfast Heaven
Watching the Chapel of Chimes funeral home
Across the street,
And through my sugar buzz–haze
The Order Of The Golden Rule in purple neon
Looked like a Man Ray Maze,
I started seein' all the sins that were buried there
Sins with grins, that they never wore
I started seein' rows and rows of dustless rooms
Perfectly manicured, to exclude the poor.

And then I started thinkin',
Maybe I should go out and buy me a coffin
Made of somethin' real natural, like pine
Something that would recycle itself
A tomb ahead of its time.
And well,

I wasn't wearing any underwear
'Cause they were still soakin' wet
I washed them and hung 'em on the line
But they weren't dry yet,
I mean, who cares, for one day.
So I'm sittin' there
With no underwear
When I feel this warm gust of wind
And the voices of angels break in
The voice of Caruso,
Greek chorus in Hi−Fi
Voices that would break Waterford crystal,
Voices that make your ears cry!

And well,
This ambush of angels,
Lift me like a fork lift
From my sugar−laced place
And they gently set me down
Right in front of the dessert display case.

Next, I'm looking face to face
With my own bloody wraith
And coffin cakes.

Well,
I reach in through the glass
And take one of the cakes
The cake called Sin City −
The shape of the universe, according to the Times
A giant chocolate Easter Egg, with many heinous crimes.
Fork lift up, out the door, across the street
And I'm in the Chapel of Chimes

I'm walkin' through the valley of the shadow of death
I'm walkin' through the valley of the shadow of death

I place Sin City on the altar slab
And say a little prayer.
Then I slowly lift my light–white linen skirt
And I lower myself down on the deadly dessert
Layers and layers of earthly delights
Lusty warrior ready for a full strength flight
Oozing cake
Slice of Sin City
Sitting cool
And looking real pretty!

CAN I HELP YOU?
CAN I HELP YOU?

I hear this voice through my bliss abyss, and
I reply:
O Bliss, and a double decker chocy coffin kiss.

THE BRAIN WASH

The only war that matters is the war against
the imagination
The only war that matters is the war against
the imagination
The only war that matters is the war against
the imagination
All other wars are subsumed in it
—Diane di Prima

Imagination Extinct
Public amnesia linked
To a pixel point idiot box screen
When radiation floods our livingrooms, bedrooms, and dens
With CNN
L.A.!!
Bringing us the play–by–play details
Of the tele–generic Disney–War
Operation Sand Box
Everyone synchronize your watches
For the Wide World of Sports, fans
            and seen on the dunes with sand in his cleats,
                    making commands, eating Oreos,
                        the well–cast, rugged,
                                but sensitive Hero
Coach Schwartzkopf, with the sand dollar tally toll,
                target control, fireworks
                            better than the Super, Super Bowl
And he says :

THEY'RE NOT P–P–PART OF THE S–S–SAME
HU–HUMAN R–R–RACE AS–AS THE R–R–REST OF US

Come on Schwartzkopf, baby, you're on a roll,
Dig your dick deep in the holy mission toy box,
For that laser−guided gang−bang thrust, that moves
the earth, when it r−r−rocks,
into Submarine sandwiches, and send them off to third world countries

Ha!!

Smart Bomb, is an Oxymoron

DEATH IN THE DARK

DEATH IN THE DARK

And from the theatre headquarters
On the stage
Bush, Reagan, whyever
On Capital Hill
Masturbating into custom−made red white and blue styrofoam cups,
Moaning

I'M THE K−K−KING OF THE C−C−CASTLE AND
YOU'RE ALL THE D−D−DIR−T−T−T−Y

Kingdom Come, in the
Championship of Testosterone.
And in the wings
F−15 after F−15
Spiritus Tartari fist−fucked by

THE LARGEST ARM−ED OFFENSIVE IN HIS−STORY
THE QUICK VIC−TORY MACHINE

Hike.

Open your boxes

Open your boxes, break the seals

Put on your gas masks

And let the birds free

Baghdad Betty's gotta lotta box
And the way she moves, and the way she talks
Ha!!
Aim and Fire, Aim and Fire, Aim and F! F! F!

Oscar Meyer Weiner test
Ketchup oozing from the end of the enemies
Nic Nac Patty Wak
Fastfood hot dog in the sky, baby
Lights, cameras, action
Dreams Deferred
Information, Ideas, Epistemology
For a New World…Odour
No bad eggs, just smart cookies

Smells like reality management to me
Swirling Fatalism
Three more waves of American Jets
The New York Mets bombing operation
Retaliate and F! F! Faster,
Smarter, Stronger,
More bionic in every way
And Where Is The Protest?
Well, there are no dead
There are No Dead

DEATH IN THE DARK
DEATH IN THE DARK

Explosions shaking the ground, and we're told
Open your boxes
Put on your gas masks
Chemical weapons attacking, but…
Ordinary telephone communications untouched
F! F! Fire

With between–the–goal–post precision
Pin–point air attack
And again, no one gets hurt
There are no dead

DEATH IN THE DARK
DEATH IN THE DARK

And to the people let it be said
That in this war there are no dead
Hype winning aspects for public support
Manufacture Gulf War Mini–Series
List all casualty in terms of Technology
Call it Patriot!
It's Perfect!

Kill the image
Kill the image

Burn the ghosts of Vietnam

DEATH IN THE DARK
DEATH IN THE DARK

Quick conquest meets organized action
And they neck

DEATH IN THE DARK
DEATH IN THE DARK

Bush actually wonders why there's so much crime on the streets of the USA
What I'd like to know,
Is how can you get tubes of crazy glue and hemorrhoid cream confused?
Anything can happen, once you shut the door and
Turn on the gas, if you're a civilian in a fallout shelter

Mis–hap Haz–ard
War with a tight deadline
Obsurd, sirens screaming
Burning, burning, burning, from the inside out

And There Are No Dead!!

Home alone, with the tree with the tiny lights
The walking dead tomorrow, unless some sleep, tonight
Sleep
United Nations only solution
Was War...
What!?
War.

DEATH IN THE DARK
DEATH IN THE DARK

And it all wrapped up like a World War II Movie
Troops marching down Broadway
High–Tech balloons making streamers across the S–S–Smog

A choir of ghosts sing with the turn of the music box key

In a War, where no one died

Peacefully.

SPLIT—SECONDS

Boots Resouled ... Destination Somewhere
Got a flat En Route to the flight
Post Departure Blues ... I arrive
Toronto

Hailed a cool cabbie in a grey fedora
I said "Pretty foggy today, too bad we can't see the sky"
He gave me one of those What—planet—you—from—lady?
Looks
And said "It's always like this"
Sorry, for thinking there's a sky.
Where there ain't no heaven there ain't no hell

Stepped into Billboard City
With too much luggage and too little to wear
Blistering cold
Barren flower beds and smoke stacks
Bridges over imbalance and earth cracks
Souls seep unleaded coffee.
Crashed at the house of the homeless
Close to the purple

Rural Robutrons and Urban Glamizons meet
At feeding time on Queen Street
To Hip Rap "How much money do you make?"
My nickname is NOBODY and I've noticed
There's no freshly squeezed anything here.
Marianne Faithfull's concert gets down, gets bad,
Gets honest, gets dirty.
Step by step I feel more and more
Like Madame Bovary on a Thursday
Am—I—her—or—is—she—me?

Can't control my hair
How can I tackle my emotions
999 right around the corner
And comments from the well–advised dwellers
"Be stone, protect yourself"
From swarming and Toronto's strangeless strangeness
Right then, The Crush
People trampling out of work
Rapid transit movement
Books with no words
Fixed to a form
Habit
To sustain a lifestyle
Somebody said would suit them
Picking up souls from the plastic surgeon
With outdated dry cleaning tags
Billy Jean, Billy Jean
Have yourself altered before you outgrow your skin
Ill–dressed dreams with an aftertaste

Time to split
Closer to the non–tolerant border the flags get bigger
Red Night Sun from the day with no shadows
Windsor
Barges divide Tumbleweed Town from Darth Vader
Detroit
Looks like a black limo with shaded windows
Pass on by
Find the heat on Kidney Street
Where the girls do a strut for boys
Bars with strobes
Reveal less clothes
And the prize goes up your nose

I was mistaken for a ghost
Strange when your first walking dead experience
Happens while still alive
Survival of the lucky
Bad etiquette of dying
Is to die without glory or a gold American Express card
Don't leave your body without it

Body pushing against the dusty air
Rolling like a tongue down the boulevard
Wind stops for an instant
And flight takes hold
53 min. in the air
Come to unrest in the Subterranean City
New York
Ground Alive
76 Stories of Density Factor Underfoot

Some guy says
"There's no crime in my area 'cause–there's–no–money"
But he's a man
Love the truth
No spitting on the bus
Homeless Homeless Homeless

And at the same time, simultaneously,
Rows of empty buildings
With broken windows
Looks like Beirut
Not all things die before they rot
How do you bury your dead
I have never seen so many full length fur coats
One woman in her F.L. fur stepped over a man
Sleeping on a vent for warmth.
Brain Photo.

I lean my head forward
Open my eyes
Garbage falls out
I have seen contamination
Water makes my skin itch
And can't find any Wheat Grass.
Snow and Crack deals fallin' down all over the place

Outside The Dakota, where Rosemary's Baby
And John Lennon were shot
Steam from Earth Nostrils blowing up
The Gothic Monster
So this is the place you end up
If you REALLY "Make It"
Ha
Blackened Catfish, Acme Hot Sauce
Say FAIZ AHMAD FAIZ!
This day Sat
Next day Sun
Market day on 79th & Columbus
Don't know why I groove it
But, I Do
Yesterday Mon
Canadada and wooooooo—wooooooo
Sleeper via Via
The mirror says I've aged six months
Looking at the world
Through the eyes of an insect.
Observation deck.
"I'm sorry man, to call Moscow you'll have to use AT&T"

I AM A CLOSET NEW YORKER

I am a closet New Yorker
Behind closed doors I sniff smog
In the shower I find myself yelling TAXI! TAXI!
I sit inside the furnace in the summertime
And sweat, I sweat like a hog
YO!
I am a closet New Yorker
Sometimes my skin turns green
In one hand I'm holding a tablet in the other a torch
And you wanna hear somethin' obscene?
I charge tourists to stand beside me
To have their pictures taken with mine
Well look, you gotta have a gimmick!
Honey, it's a sign of the times!
YO!

I said:
KEEP THEM ALLIGATORS UNDER CONTROL!
Everybody's on the dole
In one way or another
And everybody's in the hole
There's people living three stories underground
No fantasy, being a mole
YO!

I am a closet New Yorker
There are eight million people livin' in my apartment suite
Eight million people rollin' over and kickin' me in my sleep
Eight million people sittin' on the same tiolet seat
Makes me restless
Crazy man

Makes me restless
Crazy man

No wonder I never get any sleep
The moment you start to feel comfortable
You're over, you're through, you're done
As soon as you know there's a right and a left
You get confused
Like Mary
Sometimes she gets confused between TV and reality
YO!

I am a closet New Yorker
Ba—da—da—da—da
Ba—da—da—da—da
Ba—da—da—da—da
DODGE CITY!

I pack a piece when I'm here alone
I got it black market, street—beat for a measly fifty bucks
When I'm up for a buzz, I load it …
When you're alone in the alleys of your brain
There's no one to betray
Not even yourself,
If you're livin' inside your brain
As I mentioned.
Anyway,
I pretend some flim flam artist comes up behind me
And says :
UP! DON'T LOOK BACK!
Well, as you can probably tell
These lips are made for talkin'
So I turn around smooth, smooth, real smooth
I put my pistol in his pouch

And I say :
DON'T FUCK WITH A FUCK!
Sometimes I gotta get tough, when I have to
Huh!
I am a closet New Yorker
I shoot pure caffeine to stay calm
Huh!
People keep tellin' me to come out of the closet
And be the New Yorker I was meant to be
But, it's Dodge City out there
Don't they open their eyes
Don't they see
Don't they read the newspapers
Don't they watch TV
Don't they see?
It's Blade Runner times a thousand
The stone island is about to go
Only has one place to go
Seventy–six stories down into itself

BOOM!

BOOM!

BOOM!
SSSSSSSSSS
SSSSSSS
SSSS
SS
S
I

That's why there's steam comin' outta the cracks
In the sidewalks
Children in playgrounds in bullet–proof vests
Getting beat up for protection
People jumping out of buildings
Falling through awnings on the sidewalk
Lying there for nine hours
'Cause there's no one to pick up the body
Remains
Stray bullets
Everyone looking for nature identical aroma substances
Someone dies
And I go to talk to their mothers
Why?

DIANE DI PRIMA

Another third eye transmitter
Watching the fire of stillness and the rhythm and the timing
Of years of observing and participating
Of learning and experimentation
Of exploration and play
Of living.
And here I am again watching this woman
This woman, who has shared intimate moments with me
This woman, who I have loved through the words on a page
This woman
This woman.

She sits in a large comfortable chair
She asks the shadows to go away
She sips water and reads in perfect time with the order of my brain
She opens doors for me
She fans me and knees me
She takes me on a phantasy
Adventure leading me by the hand.
She brushes my hair 'til it's dry... She zaps me and makes me pour forth
sap... Straining through, through bark... She catches me in her web and
cleans my wings... White eagle... Red lion... Statue of movement... She
is Diana and she is Tara... I kneel to her ground in moon grove... And
then, with reason unknown... I slide my hand up her leg starting at her
foot... The bordeaux dress is warm... She continues reading and I con-
tinue... With my right hand extended and fingers together... Moving up
in between her knees which are pressed together... I slip my hand like
stealing a wallet from an open purse, slowly up, with control
up... Centuries burning up... Begin to feel the warmth up... And I
touch her for a moment... She unmoved continues to read... I slide my
fingers inside her and slowly move them... Love slowly circles fast vibrat-

ing grace…She reads on…Naked my body leaves me…And I become a core…Standing in the middle…Of a pear…I hold seeds inside me…The seeds become my eyes…And I hope the sun doesn't slip…Behind the morning sky…She reads…I…Listen…Can we feel?…Do we crave?…Join heat with no feeling open Bodhisattva, save…And she comes materia prima…and she kisses my forehead… Communion.

I return to my sitting…
And she continues to hum her poetry…
Hetrochromatic valium clouds…
Infinity in my hands…
She does not move…
And I realize that I want to know her…Or I just had
Something out of my control just partook my…Imagination
After the trip she brings us down slowly…
Cosmos spilling…
And I'm spilling…
Flowing in syncopation…
Bloodrush…
And the heat mist rises…
Waft of wind catches a single feather…
She floats us down…
To wake in a room of people washed…
Bringing life onto…
Breathing life into…
We leave together in magic.
She speaks to me and I can still feel
Her flight
She is Diane Di Prima
She is a magic stone that holds light

HOW DHARMA BECAME DHARMA

It all started with
What's that?
A sound
A scratching sound, at the front door
A clawing sound
Open the door, to that corner−to−corner shift
Of those running−on−empty wild cat eyes
Standing there, on the welcome mat
The Discovery of Dharma started at that moment
When the cat dashed by, in a 3G full out feline gallop
That out−of−cat breath breezed by into the inner sanctum
Where a copy of KEROUAC'S DHARMA BUMS was sitting
In the middle of the road/floor
And just like that, the cat catches the tidal−wave
And goes surfing across the hard wood floor
Surfing, with all fours on the back jacket
Of that good old Kerouac, paperback
Riding the 10−foot sutra swell curling cadi
In a per−fect nomadic per−suit
THOUGHT!
Jack's no name for that cat
And well, that's how Dharma
Became Dharma

THE MAMAS OF DADA

The Dada Mamas
Manifesto
Yes
The Mamas of Dada
The Womans Man—ifesto
Surrealling at their best—o
No more machismo manifesto
O No
The Mamas of Dada are writing their names
It's time we heard the surrealling dames, names
So the im—man—ent muse
Is never confused
And the Mamas, the sweet Mamas
Are given their do's
For their dreams and their shoes
In her—story
The Mamas of Dada
The Womans Man—ifesto
Surrealling at their best—o
No more machismo manifesto
O no
Reclaim the names that were overlooked
Within the proud pages of his—story books, hard bound
And listen to the sound
As the names of the dames, go around and around
From the lost to the found
And the flames of knowledge learn
From deep within mother ground, the orphic urn
And the candle burns
Profound, visionary
And listen to the sound

Incitionary blood it churns
And anoints the mythic wound
Omnipotent inner—flow returns
US, finally
From silence to sound:

IF IT WASN'T FOR THE MAMAS
THERE'D BE NO DADA

EILEEN AGAR
When I called the painting the Muse of Construction I wanted to emphasize the fact that although the word construction is usually associated with buildings, architecture and things mechanical, I wished to associate it with the human form which is a marvellous construction, built and assembled over millions of years, adaptable and fexible. Although its skeleton is worn inside and the soft—ware outside, it goes through many changes and holds alot of secrets in its trunk. At one time I thought of calling the painting the "Urn Goddess" as I have always been interested in the shape of a vessel, but somehow the Muse of Construction seemed more mysterious and poetic.

ANN ALPERT

MARIE—BERTHE AURENCHE

EMMY BRIDGEWATER

MARY CALDER

LEONORA CARRINGTON
I didn't have time to be anyone's muse … I was too busy rebelling against my family and learning to be an artist.

CARRINGTON
I buttered my face thickly with an electric green phosphorescent pomade. On this base, I spread tiny imitation diamonds, so as to sprinkle myself with stars like a night sky, with other pretentions.

ITHELL COLQUHOUN
I looked in and found that its distant floor was water. I began to climb down inside, taking hold of a natural bannister here, stepping on an un−hewn stair tread there, which the uneven surfaces provided. This descent was not easy, as the rock was green with damp and patched with a viscous wine−coloured growth.

LUCAS CRANACH

NUSCH ELUARD

LEONOR FINI
In Paris, Fini became a legend almost overnight. When one of the surrealists saw a painting of hers in a Paris gallery in 1936 and sought out its creator, she arranged a rendezvous in a local cafe and arrived dressed in a cardinal's scarlet robes, which she had purchased in a clothing store specializing in clerical vestments.

SUZI PERKINS HARE

VALENTINE HUGO

FRIDA KAHLO

RITA KERNN−LARSEN

GRETA KNUTSON

JACQUELINE LAMBA

DIANA BRINTON LEE

SHEILA LEGGE

DORA MAAR

JOYCE MANSOUR
Woman standing exhausted plucked
Her black legs seem in mourning for their youth
She rests her bent back against the hostile wall

Her back bent by the dreams of men
And does not see that dawn has finally broken
So long was her night.

And me I regret my madwoman's fever
I pity my degenerate parents
I would like to rub out the blood from my dreams
By abolishing maternity.

You want my belly to nourish you
You want my hair to satisfy you
You want my loins my breasts my head shaved
You want me to die slowly slowly
To murmur like a child while dying.

I will fish up your empty soul
In the coffin where your body mildews.
I will hold your empty soul.
I will tear off its beating wings
Its clotted dreams
And I will devour it.

ANN MATTA

LEE MILLER

VIOLETTE NOZIERES

MERET OPPENHEIM
Any great artist expresses the whole being.

GRACE PAILTHORPE

VALENTINE PENROSE
There is the fire it burns and I am the water I drown
O icy girl
Earth is my friend
also the moon her servant
thus we meet at the end of our caverns

GISELE PRASSINOS

The procession is composed of thirty persons. The bride precedes it, holding her recent husband by the arm. She has a huge round head furnished with a superb potato that fulfills the function of a nose. Her eyes are pierced walnuts dotted with the points of red pencils. Her mouth is very blue and she has a row of black pasty teeth. Since she is naked, you can see her body strewn with woolen tumors and her bellybutton from which hangs a little flowering dandelion. On the whole, she gives the impression of a wounded dove.

Next to her, her recent husband reaches only to her knee. He has a poor face broadened into a large smile that comes from his nose (which is in the form of a thimble and is tipped by a little navy blue button). He is clothed in a sack of green cloth that covers the top of his knees. His aluminum legs get cavities whenever he laughs. Instead of eyes he has two wilted violets. His arms are so short that in order to hold his wife he has to stop in the middle of the road. She looks at him sadly while he sings the first couplet of a song from his native land:
Diffuse Kashmir prairie
my beautiful and tender Palmyra
in your heart of wine
have a furrow of bravery
Behind them you can see the honor attendants who sing a hymn to the bride:
Wildflower
Spring rose bower
Chamberpot
Clatter.
Then comes the father of the bride with his wife buttoned to his vest.

ALICE RAHON

EDITH RIMMINGTON
From *Timetable*:
Death is alive in rhythm at the screech of the siren like a calm box pouring out music, projecting a life–time through endless rooms… In the dark tunnel above two musical boxes fight to be heard, heart against hub. On the ground the death chimneys vomit and always there is birth. When the music dies

*down life runs on wheels of search, probing for the last thought even though it
is dead. After the silence of relaxation the flower buds open, exhausted, only to
die from rhythm eaten roots. As death moves slowly oh the torture of waiting
for a new rhythm.*

KAY SAGE
The scaffolding tower is built on despair
*Sage's unpublished notebooks reveal that as early as 1955, depressed, suffering
from loss of eyesight, and unable to contemplate a future alone, she had begun
thinking about suicide. Once again, writing served as an outlet for pain and
loneliness; the poems in Demain Monsieur Silber, published in 1957, are filled
with images common to her paintings of these years. In one called Tower, she
wrote:*
> *I have built a tower on despair*
> *You hear nothing in it, there is nothing to see;*
> *There is no answer when, black on black*
> *I scream, I scream, in my ivory tower*

*And in Acrobatics, she evokes the quality of brittleness that increasingly came
to characterize her sensibility in later years:*
> *When you walk*
> *on a tight rope,*
> *at the least unexpected thing*
> *you break your neck;*
> *leave me alone*
> *I will manage*
> *all by myself*

She did not manage and on January 8, 1963 shot herself through the heart.

DOROTHEA TANNING
*If you lose a loved one does it matter if it is a brother or a sister? If you become
a parent does it matter if it is a boy or a girl? If you fall in love does it matter
(to that love) if it is a man or a woman? And if you pray does it matter, God
or Goddess?*
December 3, 1989

CLAIR DE TERRE
And in my handbag was my dream
   this smelling salt
That had only been used by the
   godmother of God.

TOYEN

REMEDIOS VARO
"Varo believed in magic," records Janet Kaplan:
She had an animistic faith in the power of objects and in the interrelatedness of
plant, animal, human, and mechanical worlds. The story is told that one
evening on a Mexican street she found a plant being sold that produced fruits
that looked like eggs. Fascinated, she brought one to her apartment, set it in the
center of her plant–filled terrace in the moonlight, and placed her tubes of paint
around it. She felt that this special plant, her paints, and the moon were
harmonious together and that their conjunction would prove auspicious for the
next day of painting.

MONIQUE WITTIG
The Eagle
I raise my rifle for practise. I see no possible target, unless I take as such the
enormous roll of sand approaching from the horizon, pushing in front of it
piles of dry branches, which are also rolled into the shape of enormous balls of
wool. Not only is the target too distant, it moves too quickly for me to plan
any line of fire. That is why I practise the rapid handling of the weapon,
grasping it with one hand, releasing the magazine with the other, reloading,
aiming, pressing the trigger, firing at random in the direction of the ochre
cloud, suddenly ceasing to fire lest the wind beats the bullet back into my face.
A desert eagle descends, circling above my head. It does not seem to be
prevented from flying by the whirling gusts of wind that blow from opposite
directions and buffet each other. Its flight is even and powerful, as is proper
for an eagle. The appearance of the eagle is all the more welcome, since I feel I
have not seen a living creature for centuries. Manastabal, my guide, does not

return. To look in the direction where she departed I glance away from the eagle, which seizes the opportunity to sweep down to the level of my face and prepare to attack me. As it is now so close to me, it is too late to level my rifle and take aim. So I content myself with firing into the air to scare the eagle away. Instead it becomes enraged and hurls itself at me, wings outspread, talons outstretched, beak open, saying:

(Cut out this stupid nonsense with your gun and your bullets, or I'll claw your face so deeply that not one of your lovers will recognize you again.)

I should like to ask it some questions, but instead I strike it on the body with my rifle—butt as hard as I can. The blow renders a hollow, metallic sound. The eagle falls to the ground with a clanking noise, its wings agitated by mechanical jerks, while the jammed automaton voice slowly repeats the same phrases:

(Whether you like it or not, Wittig, slavery has a hoarse voice. Here, you can laugh. Don't aim too bloody high, you wretched creature. Dust you were born and to dust you will return.)

The voice sticks in a screech as I kick the eagle over and over again and cry:

(Shut up, you drivelling old fool. A rolling stone gathers no moss and silence is golden.)

The robot lies at my feet, broken up, buried in the ground by its fall and my kicks, and already under the scythe—blades of the rising sands that constantly sweep over the flat surface of the desert.

Unica Zurn

Once upon a
Time a small
Once upon a time a small
warm iron was alone. No
Noise, no wine let in.
Lightly at the sea ran, while no
Ice was, thrush—pink in a
See—egg. All wink: tear
like all seeds. Sink in,

watergerm, no, alone–
in a pillow. All warmth
once upon a time's a mall.
Montpellier 1955

AND IF THEY HAVE NOT DIED
I am yours, otherwise it escapes and
wipes us into death. Sing, burn
Sun, don't die, sing, turn and
born, to turn and into Nothing is
never. The gone creates sense– or
not died have they and when
and when dead–they are not.
for H.B.
Berlin 1956

In 1960 Unica Zürn jumped to her death from a window in Bellmer's apart-
ment, fully aware that her book would soon appear.
She was seen for the last time on a bed in a morgue, her face bandaged in the
customary French manner. For the first time she had a forbidding look and
appeared extremely old.
As for her fall from the window, she had made it perfectly clear in the course
of several conversations that she lacked both the strength and the will to face
old age. She had written her books and given her testimony–before The
Jasmine Man she had published a tale from her childhood, fascinating in its
simplicity and its foreboding : "Dark Spring ends in death." And like the
twelve year old tale, the girl who was so much like her, she too jumps out of a
window – out of life – taking leave of this world because of her sense of lack :
lack of love, lack of strength, lack of knowledge.

B.R.

With fresh bed
And new pillows
I've laid the table
And I'm waiting
For you

HE WAS A HOTHEAD

He was a hothead
He blazed the night, dark
When, at times, he was a comet
He knew he was Cupid, he went straight for the heart
No compassion
He was hotheaded, he
Blazed the night, dark
He had a dream
He said he was a soldier
In Jamaica, dreamlife dreamtime
And in this dream he alone was face to face
With the evil force
And he took his gun and he erased them all
Wiped them out, at once, single handed
Then he was out of bullets
And out of the blue another gun arrives
But they were already dead
I asked what happened next
He said he woke up the next morning
Strong as a Lion
He was a hothead
Night blazed dark
She died having him
He never had a mother
So he thought that he was protected
He was surrounded with the light of death
He had so much Rum and Smoke one night
That the tire popped off his car
Lost all his windows
And settled with a shaking stomach
And a sore shoulder

He makes me yawn, when I sense his anger
His anger is deep, won't leave when he dies
He is hotheaded
He darkens night with his blaze

ON BEING A POET I

Ode to the poet in a world built on prose
    Of musing the philosophers tone
Para−normal sound surrealling around
    In−breathing supernatural funny bones

You can't be a great poet unless your heart has a break
    Which you cannot confuse with a crack
Music's a benefactor, if it's a fractal fracture
    You'll wear black and you'll never look back

But Wait!

There are no great poets, there's only great thieves
    Guess where I stole that line?
From the ancient hands of a newborn lamb
    Or off the timeless palms of an aging clochard−eh

Sublime!

Looking for the panache in the crime
    High espionage, secret agent, emissary or spy
Climbing the wall, walking the line
    Blake in your back pocket, keeping step with your time

Behind the booming doors of loves unspoken shrine
    Or out the open window of sobrieties desperate pine
For uncut ruby wine
    Prayers that speak, meditate in listen
Waiting while you're running, at the stop for a sign
    'Til you run out of the rhyme
And you're staggering thru the bushes
    Thru the dust and the brine
Feeling the bloody fall in the ruddy springtime
    O the creeping fingers of the wanton ivy vine

Seeking and peeking Onomatapoetry Divine
  For Thine!
In five–fold acrimony–harmony!

Sound that scrapes the living air
  From the trees cawing despair
Over foot, under mine
  Goes straight thru
Makes you stop on a dime
  Crow with eyes as sharp as a stone
Who speaks in a voice only myth could have known
  Squails!

Forget It
  Never Mind
Always Soul
  Jazz–er–cise your dreams
Put your passions on parole
  Mnemosyne the seven spheres
Relax your steaming ass–hole

  And!
If people ask you why you are a poet
  Say
Because it's a great excuse
  And!
If they ask you if you make a living
  Say
  Why No!
But it's Beautiful Abuse

ON BEING A POET II

Relationships are good for at least two poems
      One at the Beginning, and
      One at the End

ON BEING A POET III

When writing poems
Forget you are writing poems

ON BEING A POET IV

Poems are like warts
        They're likely to spread
As time
        They're likely to linger
Compound W will compound but the growth
        Spittle from the witch's finger...
Or a stone
        And a pond, in the water
Or a penny